INFLUENCE OF TANGO NUEVO, ETHNIC, SLAVONIAN FOLK, AND JAZZ MUSIC ON G. LIGETI'S "ETUDES POUR PIANO"

Researches, documents and hypothesis

Cristian F.D.Frattima

TABLE OF CONTENTS

Introduction:

The aim of this work is to find and prove fonts, connections and inspirations from the "non-academic" music, in the G. Ligeti's work: "Etudes pour piano". The Etudes are conventionally regrouped in 3 books, composed in the period between 1985 and 2001 and they constitute a milestone in the history of piano music and in the general field of composition. Ligeti's etudes are full of humor and imagination, and the various elements involved in the compositions include jazz, folk music, player piano as used by composer Conlon Nancarrow (1912-1997), Sub-Saharan African culture, and the musical languages of Chopin and Debussy. Complex rhythm is the central idea of Ligeti's etudes but as in all compositions of last years, there's a return to the sense of harmony.

Omitting in this writing (for shortening reasons), history and evolution of the Etude like musical genre from Scarlatti to our days, and also omitting the accurate biography and the *etapes* of Ligeti's production, we will start to treat "Etudes pour piano" as a general, short dissertation. Then we will precede writing about the "already treated fonts of influence", and conclude with our personal scientific hypothesis. Although the theorization is valid more or less for all the etudes, we will concentrate our writ on some of the most meaningful etudes, especially from the first and the second book.

CHAPTER 1: Ligeti's etudes

The 18 Etudes are arranged in three books: six Etudes in Book 1 (1985), eight in Book 2 (1988-1994), four in Book 3 (1995-2001). Ligeti wanted original to compose only twelve Etudes, "but the scope of the work grew because he enjoyed writing the pieces so much".[1] The Etudes of Book 3 are more choral-style and of a better compositional technique than those of Books 1 and 2. In Ligeti's own description of the Piano Etudes, he says, they are "Etudes in a compositional and pianistic sense" that "behave like growing organisms."[3] Upon more detailed analysis, Ligeti's complex ideas of organic structure and illusion are revealed. However, the complicated, yet highly organized configuration does not detract from poetic expression. In other words, Etudes perfectly combine virtuoso technical problems with expressive content, like rarely was done in the second half of the 20th century.

How is known, the same Ligeti admitted some of the inspiration fonts, in various interviews, but mostly in the article: "On my Etudes pour piano."[4] We will write about those in the next chapter. However, although the inspirations were many, In his Piano Etudes, Ligeti has uniquely assimilated this environment and the result is music that breathes and communicates on a personal level. Their directness of communication, innovative rhythmic texture, and virtuosic pianism place them among the most attractive and important works of contemporary piano literature.

As a matter of fact, the originality of the compositional techniques used in the 3 books is really unique: bar lines are gradually displaced, figures are methodically transposed or seemingly random rhythmic complexities are systematically introduced. Especially the Etude number two represents the first experiment of "blocked keys" in the piano history [5].

While one hand holds down various clusters (sounding them or not), the other executes very quick chromatic figures, probably impossible to human-perform at great speed, without the use of such of technique.

◆ = Depress the key silently and hold

● = Depress the key, sounding the note, and hold

●⌣◆ = Depress the key, sounding the note, and hold. The sounded note is joined on to the silent note in the next bar with a tie (even if the tone continues to sound).

Ligeti's etudes, for their innovative technique improving have been compared to Liszt's and Debussy's Etudes [6]. Although Ligeti conceived the books of Etudes as unified sets, where the original order of pieces should be respected, most of the executor doesn't perform all the cycle. The procedure of Ligeti composing the etudes was that he laid his ten fingers on the keyboard and imagines music, then his fingers copy this mental image as he presses the key[7]. He felt that the feedback between idea and tactile execution is very inaccurate, and as a result, pianists sometimes feel awkward executing some passages. As such, his pianistic approach in the etudes he composed generally follows the concepts of composers who he believes thought and composed pianistically. Here is a list of the 18 preludes with their title (Ligeti gave a title only after the composition of the musical material).

No. 1: *Désordre* – piece with polyrhythmic moving of great difficulty . **No. 2**: *Cordes à vide* – very milonga-type etude that fractaly developes itself. **No. 3**: *Touches bloquées* – one hand plays rapid successions of notes while the other hand 'blocks' some of the keys by holding them pressed. **No. 4**: *Fanfares* – an ostinato bass line for the left hand and Monk's style fragments for the right. **No. 5**: *Arc-en-ciel* – melody and harmony resembles a raimbow. The etude has many connection with Hill Evans. **No. 6**: *Automne à Varsovie* ('Autumn in Warsaw', also referring to the Warsaw Autumn, an annual festival of contemporary music) – continuous transformation of the initial descending figure, ending up at the bottom of the keyboard. **No. 7**: *Galamb Borong* – the title is in a nonsense in a Balinese-like language . It remembers the sounds of the Balinese Gamelan. **No. 8**: *Fém* – the title is the Hungarian word for metal. Is a very rhythmic etude and harmony compose itself by fifths sovrapposition. **No. 9**: *Vertige* - widely-separated hands use chromatic scales to create the effect of endless, falling movement. **No. 10**: *Der Zauberlehrling* (*The Sorcerer's Apprentice*) – a dancing melodic line is kept in perpetual motion by irregularly dispersed staccato accents. **No. 11**: *En Suspens* – six beats per bar in the right hand, four in the left hand, irregular phrase-lengths and accents in both, weave an ethereal and rather jazz-like web of harmony **No.12**: *Entrelacs* – criss-crossing rhythmic patterns, increasing in dynamics as they traverse the keyboard freom left to right, creating up to seven different metrical layers. **No. 13**: *L'escalier du diable* (*The devil's staircase*) – a hard-driving toccata that moves polymetrically up and down the keyboard and then turns into an impression of bells ringing in different registers and times **No. 14**: *Coloana infinită* (*Infinite Column*) is named for Constantin Brancusi's sculpture of the same name, a repetitive series of expanding and contracting pyramidal shapes, and features loud, ascending chord-sequences that overlap giving the impression of constant upward motion. **No. 15**: *White on White* – a white-key study except for the very end, beginning with a serene canon and with a whirling fast middle section **No. 16**: *Pour Irina* – another étude with a gentle beginning, becoming more and more frenetic due to the introduction of progressively shorter note-values and additional pitches **No. 17:** *À bout de souffle* (*Out of Breath*) – a manic two-part canon that abruptly ends with slow pianissimo chords **No. 18:** *Canon* – a short canon between the hands, played once vivace and then a second time presto possibile, with a slow quiet chordal canon.(8)

1. Richard Steinitz, *György Ligeti: Music of the Imagination* (Faber, 2003)
2. Richard Steinitz, *György Ligeti: Music of the Imagination* (Faber, 2003)
3. G.Ligeti: liner notes for *"Works for piano, volume 3: etudes, musica ricercata"* Sony classical SK 62308
4. G.Ligeti: *"On my Etudes for piano"* Sonus9, (1988)
5. In fact, the first to use the blocked keys technique was Karl-Erik Welin, on pipe organ, but we can assume Ligeti was the first to use this technique on the piano.
6. Cory Hall: *"The piano etudes of G.Ligeti"*
7. G. Ligeti *Works for Piano*. Pierre-Laurrent Aimard, Sony 01-062308-10, 1996
8. The short description of the etudes comes from "Oxford enciclopaedia of music,,

CHAPTER 2: Official inspiration fonts

Similar to every other composer who composed piano etudes in the twentieth century, Ligeti's piano etudes represent not only the pianistic virtuoso, but also a compositional sense. Ligeti combined various sources in the etudes, and most of them are associated with African rhythm, where he composed for a single player who plays several different rhythms with two hands. Ligeti's influences go beyond past and present classical composers and the traditional music of Africa and Indonesia: he has also revealed his interest in American jazz, singling out for special praise the pianists

Thelonius Monk and Bill Evans. The influences on his etudes are categorized as following:

1. His interests in African rhythm. The material in Ligeti's music of the 1980s and 90s has a strong connection with the music of sub-Saharan African cultures and can be found inthe *Études pour Piano* (1984-), Piano Concerto (1985-88), Violin Concerto (1990-92), and *Nonsense Madrigals* (1988-93). The African music and rhythm involves: "The polyphonic ensemble playing of several musicians on the xylophone – in Uganda, the Central African Republic, Malawi and other places – as well as the playing of a single performer on a lamellophone (mbira, likembe, or sanza) in Zimbabwe, the Cameroon, and many other regions.,, [8] In the above regions, Ligeti researched the technique and adapted it so he could apply it to the piano keys. He gave his

gratitude especially to ethnomusicologist Simha Aron, who developed a kind of rhythm that divides twelve beats into 3:4 ratios, as an extension of hemiola which Simha Arom called "asymmetrical internal structure"[9].

2. Hemiola. The hemiola Ligeti used is an inspiration taken from the Romantic-era piano music of Chopin and Schumann. Ligeti believed that hemiola is one of the most important elements of music from centuries ago: "I have combined two distinct musical thought processes: the meter-dependent hemiola as used by Schumann and Chopin and the additive pulsation principle of African music. Stemming from the mensural notation of the late Medieval period, hemiola arises from the metric ambiguity posed by a measure of six beats, which can be divided into three groups of two or two groups of three.

Hemiola was amongst the most popular compositional devices in the dance music of the Baroque (in the *Courante*, for example) and above all in the piano music of the 19th century."[10] Ligeti adapted African rhythm into a more complex hemiola, which Ligeti called "polytempo".This effect can be observed in the Piano Concerto (third movement) and his piano etude No.12 *Entrelacs*, pushing the hemiola concept much further. In the following chapter we will analyse the relation between Ligeti and the "Tango Nuevo" of Astor Piazzolla, composer who brought from his popular tradition, a concept of hemiola used not only for rhythmic but mostly for expressive and dramatic purposes.

3. Conlon Nancarrow's influence. The compositions for the player-piano and computer-generated images from chaos theory and fractals are ideas

that Ligeti uses in his etudes. Ligeti stated on this subject: "From his Studies for Player Piano I learned rhythmic and metric complexity. He showed that there were entire worlds of rhythmic-melodic subtleties that lay far beyond the limits that we hadrecognized in modern music until then."[11]

4. From the evidence of musical journals, concert programs, and some introductory concert remarks, the etudes are further influenced by various styles, including his own heritage – the traditions of both Western art music and his native Hungary (*Fanfares* is to be compared to Bartók's *Six Dances in Bulgarian Rhythm*); the complex metrics of Balkan music and tuning; and the "Lament motive" of descending scales that is found in many recent works. This lament motive also resembles Transylvanian funeral laments.

We will satisfactory treat this themes in the next and central chapter.

5. Modes and Tunings. Etude No.7 *Galamb Borong* demonstrates his interest in gamelan music[12], where Ligeti uses two whole-tone scales that seem influenced by Debussy's *Cloches à travers les feuilles* from the second book of *Images*. In etude No.1, *Désordre*, the technique in which one hand plays white keys and the other hand plays black keys recalls xylophone technique and the sound of Akadinda music in Uganda[13]. Jazz pianism is another important influence in Ligeti's music, as he calls for the style of jazz musicians Thelonious Monk (1917-1982) and Bill Evans

(1929-1980), this theme will be argument of treating in the next chapter.

8. G. Ligeti *Works for Piano*. Pierre-Laurrent Aimard, Sony 01-062308-10, 1996
9. Shimha Arom. *African polyphony and polyrhythm : musical structure and methodology.* (New York: Cambridge University Press, 1991)
10. G. Ligeti, *Etudes pour piano (1985), premier livre*, Volker Banfield, Wergo 60134
11. Aimard, Ligeti *Works for Piano*
12. A.Morresi *"Etudes pour Piano premiere livre di G.Ligeti: le fonti e i procedimenti,,* EDT, 2003
13. Richard Steinitz, *G. Ligeti: Music of the Imagination* (Faber, 2003)

CHAPTER 3: Hypothesis and elements of joining with *aksak, tango-nuevo, jazz and slavonian* music in some of the most meaningful etudes

Overall, Ligeti's Etudes represent a melting-pot of influences; how already written is possible to find Ethnic, Jazz and even Bulgarian and Romanian folk music elements. But in what measure the Etudes are influenced? How much are they representing a new genre in the word of academic music? This will be the question we shall try to answer in this chapter, remembering what the same G.Ligeti said: "My etudes are neither african music nor geometric fractal construction. They aren't Nancarrow but virtuoso pieces for real pianists, they are etudes in the strictest sense of the word."[14] However, like happens for all composers, influences are strong and undeniable. [15]

To understand Ligeti's cultural "microcosms" we have *in primis* to remember that G.Ligeti was born in a Hungarian Jewish family in Transylvania, Romania. After the war, Ligeti studied in Budapest under Pál Kadosa, Ferenc Farkas, Zoltán Kodály and Sándor Veres. Was very fond of ethnic music, and made many researches on Romanian folk music; briefly and worked like a teacher. In December 1956, two months after Hungarian revolution was stopped by the Soviet Army, he fled to Vienna. From that time has begin the connection with occidental music, with the jazz, the Piazzolla's tango, the ethnic African music.[16]

8. G.Ligeti: *"On my Etudes pour Piano"* Sonus9 (1988)
9. A.Einstein: *"History of music"*
10. Short Ligeti's biography from "Enciclopaedia Britannica"

3.1 First Etude: *Desordre*

Probably the technically most difficult of the Etudes, "Desordre" is an "homage to the new science of deterministic chaos."[17] The piece is harmonically static, and the bitonal elements are hardly noticed. Right hand plays white keys while left hand plays black ones. Melodically the piece is very simple, consisting of a pervasive melody, probably brought from the Hungarian folk melody *"Anya altatódal"*. The connection between the Hungarian old folk and the etude, was never declared by Ligeti, although comparing the first 16 bar of the Etude and of the melody, the bond appears undeniably:

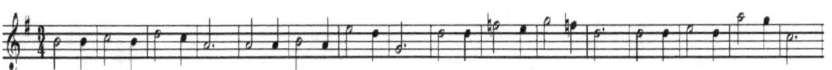

In the beginning of the piece, how is possible to deduce from the imagine, the two melodies are synchronized together, giving an impression of order; impression gradually disintegrated from the fourth bar, when the accents in the left hand start to lag behind those of right hand. The rhythmic lag grows until when the listener is not anymore able to recognize which melody leads on the other.

This kind of accent-lagging is musicologically known as "additive music", typical of Greek and balcanic folk music, probably coming from the old style of poetry reading. The *"metrica"* was the typical Greek-roman system of stressing, based on the contrast between weak accent and strong one. It was a kind of "Morse alphabet" rhythm, that doesn't contain dots or commas but just point and lines, an "indeterminate metre". Here's an example, brought from Latin poet V.Catullo's poetry production:

Fùri cùi neque sèrvus èst nequᵉ àrca
nèc cimèx nequᵉ aràneùs nequᵉ ìgnis

SCHEMA:

‒ᴗ ‒ᴗᴗ ‒ᴗ ‒ᴗ ‒ᴗ

A typical example of additive music, coming from Slavic tradition, is Igor Strawinsky's *"Dance des adolescentes"* from *"Le sacre du printemps"*:

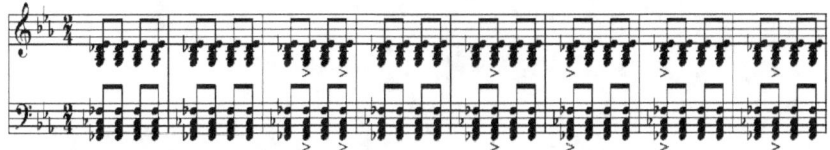

Additive schema: 4, 5, 2, 6, 3, 4, 5, 3

There's so a distinction between metre and pulsation. The bar line in Ligeti's music is only an optical aid for performers and does not give the sense of metre that it would in traditional Western music. How already written, Ligeti adapted to the piano keys, the Cameroon and Zimbabwe technique of polyrhythmic playing on lamellophone (one executor can play until three or four different rhythms,)[18] but perhaps also the Hungarian *Gypsy* style of playing the cimbalom. Remarkable in this etude is the connection with Thelonius Monk way of improvisation, with lagged accents and unpredictably, but we will speak about this element, treating etudes *Fem* and *Fanfares*.

17.   Erato, 1990

18.   G. Ligeti *Works for Piano*. Pierre-Laurrent Aimard, Sony 01-062308-10, 1996

3.2 Second etude, *Cordes a vide*

The character of this etude is less aggressive than the first one. The rhythmic is not so complex, following the only principle of hemiola (2:3, 4:6). Tempo is □=96, "Andantino rubato". The melody is counterpointed by arpeggios on the principal note (almost always the 7th or 9th of the chord) and the harmony is relatively simple, using chord of maj7 and min9[19]. Probably the most post-modernist of the etudes.

These five elements: Hemiola, Tempo Andantino rubato, arpeggios ostinato, melody type and harmony, make us speculate a formal and sound-like connection with the Argentinean Milonga.

"The milonga is a form of music which preceded the tango and the dance form which accompanies it, probably derived from an earlier style of singing known as the *payada de contrapunto*, losing the polyphonic aspect of it and becoming monadic. The milonga is generally set to an andantino 2/4 or 4/4 metre, rhythm is irregular. It is syncopated, consisting of 8 beats with accents on the 1st, (sometimes also 2nd) 4th, 5th, and 7th beats. The accompaniment is in hemiola. Harmony is mostly in minor, often using minor 9th and major 7th chords." [20] From various interviews we know that Ligeti was a great passionate of Tango and Milonga dances [21], like Igor Strawinsky, who wrote the piece "tango" in 1940 and orchestrated it for chamber orchestra in 1953. Here is a comparison between *Cordes a vide* and a milonga.

Astor Piazzolla, fragment from "Oblivion" 1974

G.Ligeti, fragment from second Prelude: Cordes a vide, 1985

19. Eric Drott analyzed the harmonic structure of this prelude in the book: *"The role of Triadic harmony"*
20. *"Tango! The Dance, the Song, the Story"*. Collier, Cooper, Azzi and Martin. 1995. Thames and Hudson, Ltd
21. *"G. Ligeti in Conversation with Péter Várnai, Josef Häusler, Claude Samuel and himself"*. (London:Ernest Eulenburg Ltd 1983)

3.3 Third etude, *Touches bloquees*

Another perpetual motion etude, the constant quaver pattern that one plays is incongruent with that one hears. The title *Blocked keys* how we already wrote about, refers to a very interesting pianistic technique whereby one hand plays a rapid even succession of notes in a chromatic scale while the other hand blocks prescribed keys by keeping them silently depressed, affecting the rhythm pattern. The result is a series of complicated patterns that appear chaotic.

For obvious reasons, is not possible to find connections with folk or tango music in this etude, but is quite evident the connection with *bebop* jazz, and so with Thelonius Monk, Ligeti's favorite jazz pianist.

The connection with this pianist is clearer in the fourth and eight etudes. Monk's ways of improvisation was "differently logic", and rich of *ghost notes. Ghost notes* are in the jazz language, not played or partially played sounds that our mind imagines and figures like logic phrase notes, but our ear cannot effectively ear. Wind instruments, human voice, and guitars are examples of instruments generally capable of ghosting notes without making them synonymous with rests, while a pianist or percussionist would have more difficulty in creating this distinction because of the percussive nature of the instruments, which hampers the resolution of the volume gradient as one approaches silence. For this reason Ligeti's third etude technique, greatly simplify the possibility to achieve difficult and chaotically accented patterns. In the picture, a famous blues of the *bebop* saxophonist Charlie Parker, "Au privave".

With x are represented the ghost notes, according the jazz "pronounce" of the great bebopist. The connection between Ligeti's etude and the ghost note concept is still not scientifically conjectured, but still very interesting feature.

3.4 Fourth and Eight etudes: *Fanfares* and *Fem*

In this paragraph we are going to treat the *jazzy* and *aksak* character of two among the most meaningful etudes: *Fanfares* and *Fem,* we shall also argument the strict relation between the two etudes.

Fanfares is one of the most frequently performed etudes among Ligeti's ones. The perpetual ostinato, which is repeated 208 times with only octave transpositions, is the most distinct feature of this piece. The perpetual motion throughout the piece is reminiscent of Bartok's *Six Dances in Bulgarian Rhythm.*

B.Bartók: *Six Dances in Bulgarian Rhythm*

G.Ligeti: Fourth Etude *"Fanfares"*

The *aksak* character of the ostinato that combines with the melody of another part reveals both Ligeti's Hungarian influence and his obsession with polymetrics. But what means *aksak?* *Aksak*, defined by Encyclopædia Britannica, is a Bulgarian Rhythm, a variety of musical metre characterized by combinations of unequal units of beats, such as 2 plus 3 or 3 plus 2 and their extensions. Thus 3 + 3 + 2, or 2 + 3 + 3, produces 8/8 units quite unlike the 4/4 common to Western music. As non-Western music, began to exert influence in the West, *aksak* rhythms found their way into the works of a number of 20th-century composers of Western art music, Bartók and Stravinsky foremost among them. This unequal units of beats, producing 8/8, is also an important feature of tango music, always containing 3+3+2 or 3+2+3 against 4/4, but in this case is conceivable only a far font connection with Argentine music. The rhythmic feature is also similar to the Transylvanian dance *mocanesc* (3+2+3).

Anyway the title *fanfares,* suggests a folk Slavic brass formation. *Fem* is a Hungarian word indicating a bright metal. The etude is characterized by an African pygmies *clave*, very similar to a *Cakewalk* or *Rag-time*[22] syncopated rhythm, and like in *rag-time*, chords are formed by two couples of fifths:

G. Ligeti, 4th etude, Fem

In fact, the 12/8 metre chosen by Ligeti is more a 4+4+4 then a traditional western 3+3+3+3.If rewriting the first 3 bars in 2/4, to represent the clave in conventional way...:

...we can simply find out a cicle of nine bars, repeated very often in the devoloping of the piece. So, rewriting the first nine bars in 2/4, and conventionally giving the fictitious tonality of Db we can recognize the big similarity with *rag* music:

This similarity is absolutely not denied by Ligeti, who wrote as performing indications for this etude: "Play very rhythmically and springy, with swing, use pedal sparingly.,, The spare use of pedal, like in jazz music, is another clear evidence of the massive influence that jazz pianism has on this etude. Finally, Ligeti gives a very strong prove of jazz fonting in the last part of the etudes: he not only concludes the piece with a pianissimo section in dotted quarts in which the *groove* improvisely stops, remembering the Chikago-style finals of Duke Ellington, Charlie Mingus and Benny Golson, but even places like *cadenza* (ending), a couple of "pure-jazz-voicing,, chords:

In both etudes, *fanfares* and *fem*, is possible anyway to distilled recognize Thelonius Monk's[23] eccentric, angular style of improvisation. "Fanfares, has passages where first the right hand, and then the left, play Monk-like short, zany improvisatory fragments while the other hand accompanies with a series of eight quirky running notes that repeat in a short loop much in the nature of a "vamp"   figure   in   jazz."[24]

Thelonius Monk: Improvisation fragment from "Epistrophy". T.Monk quartet, Paris, 1966

Thelonius Monk: Intro from "Brilliant corners,,

1957

22. **Cakewalk** is a pre-ragtime dance form popular until about 1904. The music is intended to be representative of an African-American dance contest in which the prize is a cake. The metric cycle is circular and irregular, strongly polyrhythmic structure. **Ragtime** (alternately spelled **rag-time**) is an original musical genre which enjoyed its peak popularity between 1897 and 1918. Its main characteristic trait is its syncopated, or "ragged," rhythm. It began as dance music in the red-light districts of American cities such as St. Louis and New Orleans years before being published as popular sheet music for piano. It was a modification of the march made popular by John Philip Sousa, with additional polyrhythms coming from African music. Ragtime influenced Classical composers including Debussy and Stravinsky. (Enciclopaedia Britannica)

23. **Thelonious Sphere Monk** (October 10, 1917 – February 17, 1982) was an American jazz pianist and composer considered "one of the giants of American music". Monk had a unique improvisational style and made numerous contributions to the standard jazz repertoire. Monk is the second most recorded jazz composer after Duke Ellington, Often regarded as a founder of bebop, Monk's playing later evolved away from that style. His compositions and improvisations are full of dissonant harmonies and angular melodic twists, and are consistent with Monk's unorthodox approach to the piano, which combined a highly percussive attack with abrupt, dramatic use of silences and hesitations. (Richard Cook and Brian Morton: *"The Penguin Guide to Jazz", 2008, London*

24. A.Morresi: "Il primo libro di studi di G.Ligeti, le fonti e I procedimenti". EDT 2003

3.5 Fifth Etude, *Arc-en-ciel*

Etude No.5 portrays its title by a rhythmic texture comprised of many strands and by a descending chromatic figure. Embedded in its tempo indication is another reference to jazz with the instruction: "with swing". Also Ligeti footnotes the opening measure: "Varying tempo: the metronome mark represents an average, the semiquaver movement fluctuating freely

around this average tempo, like in jazz." Harmonically the piece consists almost entirely of seventh and minor ninth chords, and one of the most striking features is the use of a major-seventh chord followed by a minor-seventh or ninth chord, creating descending parallel fifths[25]. The most distinctive character of Ligeti's fifth etude *Arc-en-ciel* is its *"Bill Evans,,* [26] massive influence. Evans's innovative voicing creates exquisite sounds and has influenced many jazz pianists. He did not say much about jazz theory, but expressed his thought simply through his playing. He employed innovative voicings based on his classical training. This includes his sensitivity in differentiating tone qualities between voices, controlling the phrases of contrapuntal lines, and his experiments in altering melodies. He brought an unusual harmonic idiom to jazz, among them, his distinctive voicing and rootless chords.

Most important, his voicing, tone quality, and harmonies are reminiscent of several classical composers including Debussy and Ravel, with something like Brahms's melodic lines on the left hand, and an infusion of bird sounds similar to Olivier Messiaen (1908-1992)'s music. The harmonies in *Arc-en-ciel* reflect Evans's rootless voicing, and most of the time Ligeti stays in a higher position suggesting elegant gestures like Evans' music. Also, four contrapuntal lines are laid out clearly, exactely like in Bill's polyphony idea. An important aspect to be treated is the internal structure rhythm. This etude streams with consecutive sixteenth notes in four different types of rhythm, two in the right hand and two in the left hand.

Subdivision is provided that divides a measure in the treble part into three, while the bass part is divided into two . This element of twelve-beat groups divided into 3:4 patterns is typical of bebop, but also of tango and milonga music, cause of the common African root. The ethnomusicologist Aron called this polyrhythmic element: "asymmetrical internal structures".[27]

G.Ligeti:5thetude:*Arc-en-ciel*

A.Piazzolla: "Milonga del angel"

The other component of this etude is the lament motive that also occurs in the etude *Automne à Varsovie*. The lament motive consists of descending chromatic lines that are often associated with expressions of grief and sadness. The following figure illustrates the first three phrases in the top voice of *Arc-en-ciel*:

Steinitz described that the basic characteristics of Lament motive in Ligeti's recent music includes:

1. It is a three-phrase melody of which the third is longer in duration.

2. Each phrase mainly descends in semitones, but with occasional upward leaps.

3. Each phrase ends lower and/or starts higher than its predecessor.

4. Notes of greater expressive significance are often intensified harmonically by major sevenths.

5. Rhythmically, the phrases present a basic value which is doubled or tripled at
important points.

This lament motive resembles Transylvanian funeral songs[28]. Shockingly similar is the Romanian lament for a child *"Bocet la fecior"*:

Romanian Funeral lament: *"Bocet la fecior"*

Lament notes schema in Ligeti's fifth etude

Another etude with swing approach, jazz chords, polyrhythm and Evans voicing is the 11th, *"En suspens"*, maybe the most post-modernist of all Etudes. The tempo marking is "Andante con moto, avec l'elegance du swing". It's very colorful and *vaudeville* tasty.

25. Cory Hall: *"The Piano Etudes of G. Ligeti"*, Book1
26. **William John Evans**, known as **Bill Evans** (August 16, 1929 – September 15, 1980) was an American jazz pianist. His use of impressionist harmony, inventive interpretation of traditional jazz repertoire, and trademark rhythmically independent, "singing" melodic lines influenced a generation of pianists including: Chick Corea, Keith Jarret, Herbie Hancock. Evans studied classical piano when he was young, and his classical music background enhanced his pianistic technique and other aspects in his jazz improvisation. (Simpson Joel, B.Evans biography)
27. Shimha Arom. *African polyphon and polyrhythm : musical structure and methodology.* (New York: Cambridge press,1991)
28. About romanian funeral traditions: http://www.culturalromtour.com/sites-in-romania_romanian-funeral-traditions_19.html

3.5 Fourteenth and Fifteenth etudes: *White on white* and *Pour Irina*

Two among last Ligeti's etudes, reflect a changed composition style in the composer, a great interest for the popular choral music, for the Charlie Mingus' composition "suite-like" and for a light, elegant and very rare modal harmony. By the way, an accurate mathematic analysis would show a "fractal" structure: a very simple half notes or quarter notes melody goes complicating itself until a very dense musical tissue, but we will not deepen this theme in this dissertation. What is interesting to show is the relation between *White on White*, and its melodic derivation from a traditional Hungarian melody, like it's shown in the comparation:

Ligeti's 11th etude "White on White" and the traditional Hungarian song: *"Nosztalgia"*

Is also remarkable in the last preludes, the abandon of triadic and 7th chord system, and the use of diatonic modality. In the precise case of 11th etude, Aeolian mode. We can only conjecture (for the absence of literature) a probable influence of one of Ligeti's favorite jazzmen: Keith Jarrett with his linear modal simple improvisation style. Concluding, we like to see a probable connection of the etude *Pour Irina,* with Bill Evan's *"Pour Nenette".* The conjecture is only far, but the beginning quarter rhythm peace broken by phrasing rests, the sad esatonic doric scale, the fractal structure remembering Evans' improvisation, make the conjecture not poor of evidences:

B.Evans' *"For Nenette"* beginning section

G,Ligeti's *"Pour Irina"* central section

CONCLUSIONS

"Fonts are many, but my etudes are neither African music nor geometric fractal construction. They aren't Nancarrow but virtuoso pieces for real pianists; they are etudes in the strictest sense of the word."

"My rejection of *avant-garde* music also lays me open to attacks and accusations of being a postmodern composer. I don't give a damn. I'm a composer of the future, who looks with nostalgia to his past"

György Ligeti in Conversation with Péter Várnai, Josef Häusler, Claude Samuel and himself. (London: Ernest Eulenburg Ltd 1983).

BIBLIOGRAPHY

- Arom, Simha. *"African Polyphony and Polyrhythm: Musical Structure and Methodology. „* Translated by Martin Thom, Barbara Tuckett, and Raymond Boyd.
  New York: Cambridge University Press, 1991.
- Review of *„György Ligeti: Music of the Imagination"*, by Richard Steinitz. *Notes* 60 (March 03, 2004).
- Drott, Eric. *"The Role of Triadic Harmony in Ligeti's Recent Music."* Music Analysis
  22, no.3 (2003).
- Hall, Cory. *"The Piano Etudes* of György Ligeti, Book 1." DMA diss., University of Kansas, (1994).
- Ligeti, György. *"On My Etudes for Piano."* Translated by Sid McLauchlan. *Sonus* 9, no.1 (1988).
- Steinitz, Richard *"György Ligeti: Music of the Imagination,,* Boston: Northeastern University Press, 2003
- A.Morresi *"Etudes pour Piano premiere livre di G.Ligeti: le fonti e i procedimenti. „* EDT, 2003
- *György Ligeti in Conversation with Péter Várnai, Josef Häusler,*
- *Claude Samuel and himself.* (London:Ernest Eulenburg Ltd 1983).
- *"The Penguin Guide to Jazz",* 2008, London
- *"Tango! The Dance, the Song, the Story".* Collier, Cooper, Azzi and Martin. 1995. Thames and Hudson, Ltd